Find Out What Has Been Missing From Mainstream Purpose Education

….When you do, don't be surprised if you discover your own personal power, fulfillment and joy for life and living!

Opening yourself to the full understanding and meaning of purpose can be a game-changer for how you feel about yourself and life.

This book will help you set a powerful course of opening yourself to the world of purpose from a full mind-body-spirit perspective. Not only will you gain clarity about your purpose, but you will also be given tools that will greatly assist you in removing blocks that have held you back in the past.

Don't waste another minute of your life lingering in the dark! Get illuminated and get going on your amazing path that was designed specifically for you. Obtain:

- The secrets that most people miss about purpose
- 6 Specific Steps for gaining clarity about your purpose
- Effective tools that aide you in your journey

Pick up a copy of this powerful book today and begin moving with greater clarity towards your exhilarating, inspiring and fulfilling life!

Your Amazing Itty Bitty® **Purpose Book**

15 Things Adults & Teens Must Know for Finding & Aligning With Their Purpose

Gretchen E. Downey
1 Best Selling Author

Published by Itty Bitty® Publishing
A subsidiary of S & P Productions, Inc.

Copyright © 2015 Gretchen E. Downey

All rights reserved. No part of this book may be reproduced or transmitted in any form or by any means, electronic or mechanical, including photocopying, recording or by any information storage and retrieval system, without written permission of the publisher, except for inclusion of brief quotations in a review.

Printed in the United States of America

Itty Bitty® Publishing
311 Main Street, Suite D
El Segundo, CA 90245
(310) 640-8885

ISBN: 978-0-9987597-3-9

This book is dedicated to our human family. Let us work together and support both our personal and collective upward development. As we elevate ourselves, we elevate the entire consciousness of the planet. For one cannot happen without the other… as we are intricately connected to each other. Invite yourself to lay down your thoughts of separation, differences and disempowerment. Then do your part to elevate your own internal landscape…. and that of the world around you.

Wishing you blessings and joy on your journey of this exhilarating and magical thing called life!

*"You are perfect as you are…
and becoming more every day."*

Stop by our Itty Bitty® Publishing website for more exciting information about finding your purpose and parenting.

www.ittybittypublishing.com

For more books and information on conscious parenting from this author, visit:

www.thekidwhisper.com

Looking for great tools and strategies for parenting teens? Get Gretchen Downey's **#1 Best-Selling Itty Bitty Book, "Parenting Teens – 15 Powerful Strategies for Understanding How Your Teen Thinks"** to gain a better understanding of how the teen mind and brain works and how to effectively fortify their upward development during this transformational period of life.

Table of Contents

Introduction
Item 1. Why You Are Here?
Item 2. The Anatomy of Purpose
Item 3. Step #1 - What is My Greatest Desire
Item 4. Step #2 - What Do I Lack The Most?
Item 5. Step #3 - What is My Greatest Talent?
Item 6. Step #4 - What Lessons Am I Applying?
Item 7. Step #5 - What Lessons Have I Been Taught?
Item 8. Step #6 - What is My Purpose in Life and What Do I Have to Share?
Item 9. Anatomy of Teen Purpose
Item 10. Teens & Adult Purpose – Differences
Item 11. You Are Not Your Emotions
Item 12. Beliefs & Imprints – Activating Internal Cooperation & Realignment
Item 13. How to Get Into Alignment With Your Higher Self
Item 14. The Roadblock to Your Greatness
Item 15. Getting Organized

Introduction

In this Itty Bitty® Book you will find 15 simple, yet powerful things you can do to more fully understand your purpose.

Purpose is often a very misunderstood topic. Why? Because, most people are only looking at one aspect of purpose, which usually consists of the subject of providing service or goal setting (i.e., finding what you're good at and then making a goal of sharing it with the world). While this is a noble and worthy aspect of purpose, it's not the entire picture! For starters, ***purpose is not a goal***. Goals simply help you organize yourself to complete a task. Human purpose is always two-fold.

First, is your *"primary purpose,"* which is about connecting with your Soul and discovering what you were called to *do* and *be* at the very core of your being. It consists of: 1) the *deepest desire* of what or how your Soul (spiritual nature) wants you to contribute to the world in this lifetime and 2) the *inner work* that you do to evolve into higher and more improved version of yourself.

Second is your *"secondary purpose,"* which relates to the expression of your primary purpose within your physical world and relationships. It's the activities and actions that you carry out in your physical life that relate to your primary purpose. It's the use of your endowed skills and talents to build a better world.

We operate in an evolving Universe. Nothing stays the same – including you. Part of your purpose is to grow into a higher human being in how you think, feel and act ~ and then to spread this goodness into the world through your gifts and talents.

So many human beings feel lost, unfulfilled or like something is missing – and this needn't be the case at all! True fulfillment and joy will continue to elude all of us until we connect with our Soul's desires for us ~ and then radiate this beautiful aspect of ourselves from within…and outwardly into the world.

The greater part of purpose is the inward development and commitment to overcoming our limiting beliefs, behavior patterns, thoughts and actions that hold us back from becoming the limitless beings that we were born to be! Solving the world's problems without addressing what's going on *inside* ourselves will only keep us in a holding pattern of unfulfillment and lack.

Life will always nudge you if you aren't listening to your Soul's calling. Therefore, step with ease into a greater understanding of yourself. When you do, you will move more joyfully and effortlessly with the stride of your own life!

Item 1
Why Are You Here?

Each of us has a reason for being here and for experiencing this extraordinary thing called *life*. Each human being has 3 parts to their human construction or constitution – a mind, body and a spirit. The latter is the highest aspect of your nature and it is the all-knowing and all-seeing aspect of yourself. Unfortunately most people only identify with their physical nature – the body. Your primary purpose is to connect with your Soul and operate from the desires it has for you and your life. What you need to understand:

1. Everyone born on this planet came to serve a purpose. No two persons are alike. When we embrace this consciousness and understanding, we will stop competing with one another and begin working **with** each other and ***in service of*** one another.
2. There is no competition for your purpose. It was contracted to you alone by the Divine – or any name you use for God.
3. Your Soul knows the reason you are here and the blueprint of your life. You must discover what that is.
4. Part of your purpose involves discovering your own power and human potential.
5. A common purpose that each human has is to be a responsible caretaker of Earth.

What Purpose Isn't

- It's not a task that needs to be completed.
- It's not a goal.
- Not a destination – *Your Soul's primary purpose doesn't change but your physical experiences and learning continually evolve.*
- It's not something you find – you already have it. Your Soul knows the secrets of your purpose. You only need to unveil it.
- It's not a fleeting novelty – it is some-thing sacred, unique and personal to you.

What Purpose Is

- A catalyst for giving your life fulfillment, joy, inspiration, love and meaning…both for you and for all other life forms.
- Something which supports your own individual human learning, potential and growth – while also supporting that of others.
- It's a journey of service and contribution to the *collective whole*.
- A journey of personal expansion.
- An aid that helps you recognize your own individual and collective power.
- A "binder" that glues humanity together and helps reconnect us to our **unity** and **oneness** – and that each of us are essential for changing the course and direction of our planet in a unified way.

Item 2
The Anatomy of Purpose

Your #1 Primary Purpose is to find and connect with your Soul's desires for you. Your soul has a code, a blueprint, for what you are here to do during your physical lifetime and it wants this to be fulfilled. Your only job is to figure out what it is…and live and operate from it. Things to know:

1. The reason so many of us feel unhappy, uninspired or like something is "missing" is because we are off target or misaligned with our own blueprint or Soul's purpose.
2. The sparkle of life will forever remain illusive until a person commits to living from this endeavor.
3. Your Soul's *primary purpose* doesn't change, but your life experiences and learning do. The unending variety of the latter always brings you closer to the full expression of your primary purpose.

To link with your purpose you must be able to listen to your heart. Ask your heart (not your head) some of the following questions.

1. What is precious to me?
2. What do I trust; what makes me feel (authentically) good?
3. What motivates and inspires me?
4. What nurtures and nourishes me?
5. What do I love or love doing/expressing?

Preparation Exercise for Next 6 Chapters

It's important to get yourself into a happy, peaceful frame of mind and free of time commitments while you're doing the "6 Steps" in the following chapters. Think of it as sacred time with your Inner Self. Take several days or weeks if you need to. For some, this may be an ongoing revelation process. Do the following pre-meditation exercise slowly to prepare you.

- Find a quiet, peaceful place. Sit comfortably upright. Quiet your mind and center yourself by closing your eyes. Take 3 slow full deep breaths, *in through the nose and out through the mouth.*
- Imagine a beautiful white beam of light coming from the highest point in the Universe, moving down through the crown of your head, traveling through your brain, spinal column, out the sacrum, through the chair/floor and deep into the center of the earth.
- Move your attention to your heart center and prepare to lovingly clear it. Ask and release the following:
    - What do I have to forgive (release) about myself? What are the reasons for not acknowledging my own goodness and light? (Then repeat this for others).
    - Bless all that is around you, knowing that it is creating a better world.

Item 3
Step #1 – What is My Greatest Desire

Read through the ***entire*** chapter before beginning the exercises within each of the 6 Steps. While focusing on your heart center (not your head or mind), ask yourself, *"What is my greatest heart's desire?"* The following suggestions will help you stay focused. Release any ideas about:

1. Rushing – It's slow, self-reflective.
2. Judgment of the desire or yourself.
3. What others think about your desire or what you "should" do or be able to do.
4. Limitations or the thought that something can't be done. This is THE big one!
5. How a desire will provide income, make money or satisfy a temporary material want. Your *heart's desire* is a *Soul goal or desire*, materiality is insignificant to it.

Here are things you can do to cultivate clarity about your heart's desire. Reflect on each slowly.

1. Feel the internal excitement you'd feel if your desire came true. This is not a materialistic desire for an object(s) – although something may manifest physically as a result of your desire.
2. Feel the love and benefit your desire has for yourself and others.
3. Dissolve all limitations and ask your heart "What do I long to do or be?"

Examples

Here are a few examples of a heart's desire. Do not try to duplicate these. They are only to stimulate your thinking. Be sure to reflect only upon your own life to come up with your own unique answers. There is no wrong or right – only what is right for you!

- Live in a state of joy - no matter what life is presenting.
- To master the art of forgiveness.
- Be of service to… (e.g., children).
- To master and share faith instead of fear.
- To overcome "lack" consciousness or to know that I AM abundance.
- To unconditionally love or accept myself.
- To know inner peace and serenity and live in alignment with both.

To Do:

- Begin with the "centering exercise" to quiet the mind and bring forth your Higher Self.
- Take time working through this step. Get a notebook or notecards to take notes. Write down thoughts and ideas about each of your heart's desires. As you assemble the information, reflect upon your answers and prioritize your top three items.
- If able, narrow it to one item that propels and drives you at the core of your being.

Item 4
Step #2 – What Do I Lack The Most?

This is a highly significant step. Contrary to what many might incorrectly perceive as negative, this step is extremely important and necessary for developing your human potential and advancing your evolution! Those that possess the wisdom and courage to *look at and confront* their limiting (negative) beliefs and behaviors squarely head-on, are those who continually and **rapidly catapult** themselves upward in their personal growth, evolution and consciousness.

The following are questions you can ask yourself or ways to gain clarity about Step #2. Remember to do the centering activity from Item 2 to bring forth your Higher Self before you begin.

1. What is missing in my life at some level or has always been missing in my life?
2. What characteristic(s) is missing from my human constitution and/or personality that keeps tripping me up over and over? For example, do I lack self-confidence, and as a result, allow people in my life to treat me like I'm not important?
3. What have close friends or family lovingly pointed out to me over the years - these are clues to my opportunities.
4. Release and detach from all judgment of yourself or the answers you receive.

Examples

The following are examples of what others commonly feel they "lack the most." It's important to note that Steps 1 & 2 are often close opposites of one another. What you lack can often be what your heart desires.

- Honesty, forgiveness
- Faith, fortitude, discernment
- Confidence, or belief in myself or God
- Empowerment or belief in my greatness
- Love and acceptance toward others, or self
- Compassion toward others, or self
- Joy, kindness, understanding, peace
- Worthiness, appreciation, gratitude

To Do:

- Begin with the "centering exercise" to quiet the mind and bring forth your Higher Self.
- Take extra time working through this step. Get a notebook or notecards to write down each item that comes to you.
- If you get an emotional response or feelings of self-judgment, breathe deeply and exhale any negative emotions as you write down your answers and ideas.
- If needed, prior to beginning this Step 2 you may jump ahead and read Item 11 to help you better understand emotions and how they work.

Item 5
Step #3 – What is My Greatest Talent?

You are unique and specifically equipped with many useful talents that help you navigate life while serving your important purpose and life's work. Talents are what allow us to create and help us express our Soul's desire and purpose during our lifetime.

1. Observe yourself from many perspectives – not just from what your family, friends or teachers tell you you're good at. Go inside and let your Higher Self tell you your talents.
2. Release judgment of yourself or your talents.
3. Release the need to let society, social and cultural norms influence your thoughts about the value of your talents.
4. Think big, broad and out of the box! Really give yourself credit for those talents that others or society don't value or pay attention to! These are golden!
5. No talent is too big or too small. They all serve a purpose in the grand scheme of creating the unique YOU!
6. Include talents that you may have suppressed or others incorrectly labeled as flaws. For example, were you always acting silly in class as a kid? It may have gotten you into trouble, but you added levity and smiles to the world!

Examples

The following are examples of talents. It's important to note that talents do not necessarily express themselves the same way in all people. When a talent is not appropriately managed, it can become a hindrance. Every person must learn to regulate and find equilibrium in maintaining the "best" expression of his or her talents.

- Willful or strong-willed, talkative.
- Easily get people to "lighten up" or promote levity instead of stress.
- Loving, kind, compassionate, empathetic, joyful, beautiful, humble.
- Easily sees through lies or illusions; wise and/or understanding: forgiving or easily releases resentments, anger/frustrations.
- The "glue" - i.e., inclusive, unify people, dissolve boundaries and bridge diversity.
- Full of physical and/or emotional strength, sensitivity and/or gentleness.

To Do:

- Begin with the "centering exercise" to quiet the mind and bring forth your Higher Self.
- Take extra time working through this step. Write down each item on notecards.
- Identify your top 3-5 talents. Reflect on your entire list often – all are valuable assets that serve your mission! And, you will add more as you grow and change!

Item 6
Step #4 – What Lessons Am I Applying?

This step is all about what you are *currently* learning and/or continue to struggle with. These are lessons and experiences comprising your current reality and life's focus. View these as a *"shorter term"* purpose work. They will change as you master and transcend them, unlike your life-long purpose, which doesn't change. They may however, take a lifetime to master if you don't do the work. They can include things like:

1. What lessons keep crossing my path over and over that remain unresolved, cause me problems or keep me stuck?
2. Experiences big or benign – even if they seem small, they can still be influential in the grand scheme of your life.
3. Include lessons that are both joyful and painful. Leave no stone unturned. Your answers are clues to your *primary purpose*, your Soul's advancement and your evolution! That's triple the rewards for a single effort. **You will pay yourself in spades by focusing your efforts on Step #4.**
4. Revisit this step on a regular and annual basis.

Examples

Here are just a few examples to stimulate your creative thinking and perspective.

- How to see the good in things and people.
- Overcoming "lack" mentality.
- How to take responsibility for myself and actions, or change repetitive patterns that keep showing up in my life.
- Overcoming gossip, drama, resentment, anger, reactivity, shyness, pessimism, stress, dishonesty, criticism, judgment.
- How to take charge of motivating myself.
- Finding and maintaining joy from within.
- Having faith, confidence, and courage.
- How to be a good friend; loyalty.
- Commit to caring for my body and health.
- How to love my body or myself more.
- Forgive myself and/or others.
- How to be non-judgmental; more accepting, inclusive and/or appreciate diversity.

Recommendations:

- Begin with the "centering exercise" to quiet the mind and bring forth your Higher Self.
- Obtain several note cards and lay out each item identified on a single card.
- Look for links between the other Steps that you've completed and will complete in future chapters.

Item 7
Step #5 – What Lessons Have I Been Taught?

This step is all about what you've learned thus far from your life experiences, which has brought you to this point in your life. It will include items that you have worked on and transformed. This learning is used to support your purpose work. Ask yourself the following questions.

1. What have the lessons I've learned shown me? What truths and lies about my thinking have they exposed?
2. How have they advanced my thinking, acting and speaking? What's next?
3. Do I have improved emotional responses or regulation as a result of my learning?
4. Are my perceptions more accurate now and in alignment with my Higher Self?

Ensure that you are reflecting upon the truly beneficial side of your life lessons and learning. Remember, everything and every situation has a silver lining. If you are focusing solely upon the negative aspects of a life's lessons, then you are off track and these items belong in Step #2 or #4. For example:

1. I've learned that I will always put me first from now on! Forget everyone else!
2. I can't trust anybody.
3. I will do whatever it takes to get ahead.

Examples

The following are examples of applied lessons. Take notice if some of your examples show up in other Steps. These reoccurrences are strong indicators that provide direction to either your primary or secondary purpose work.

- Ability to have faith; i.e., you may have acquired the ability to have faith in your children, but may still be working on all other areas of your life. This may even belong in Step #1 – your heart's desire.
- I really can stop criticizing others, and lift them up instead. Putting others down doesn't make me more powerful – it reveals to me my insecurities to work on.
- I realize that I'm more powerful than I thought. I can accomplish...
- I changed an old belief pattern of...

To Do:

- Begin with the "centering exercise" to quiet the mind.
- Take extra time working through this step. Get a notebook or notecards to write down each item that comes to you.
- Be thorough in your observations of all the things you've accomplished, both short and long-range. Remember, *you are a masterpiece and a work in progress*. Honoring your progress in love sets you up for greater awareness and future growth!

Item 8
Step #6 – What is My Purpose in Life and What Do I Have to Share?

It's now time to assemble your information.

1. Place your notecards from each step side-by-side or record your findings on a separate sheet of paper.
2. Take notice of any links or similarities.
3. Notice any areas that are opposites or opposing. For example, your heart's desire is to be a peacemaker and you notice themes of drama, gossip and stress have been showing up in other steps.
4. Take your time and trust your intuition! There may be areas your ego doesn't want you to face. Your Higher Self, however, may be giving you strong messages that it's time to address these! **Those giving you trouble and pain are the areas that your Soul is inviting and encouraging you to change.**
5. Remember, purpose is two-fold. It's about sharing your gifts with the world and it is about your own personal growth. These two *must* be in balance. We can never truly be fulfilled unless we address both. Which areas are you ignoring? Do you find it harder to look in the mirror or to unconditionally love or give to others?

Important Tips to Clarify Your Purpose.

- *Talents help me with what I'm missing.* They bolster me to overcome each life lesson that I'm applying (or limitation that I'm going to overcome).
- *Talents are the tools by which I fulfill my heart's desire.* Use and share all of them generously and unconditionally! Put them to right use…in the right situation. Not all talents should be used at all times.
- *My deepest sense of lack is the area I came to overcome.* This can be within myself and/or outwardly towards others.
- The primary purpose of your soul is to guide you to **seek** and **share** its Light and help you remember that you are a beautiful, powerful and benevolent spark of the Creator. Your spiritual growth always benefits from your physical experiences.

Rules of thumb:

- If I am not functioning within my target, my soul will do everything it can to get my attention and drive me toward my purpose.
- The less I listen, the more discomfort, unfullfillment and pain I will feel. *Pain is the only motivation the soul has to get me to correct how I think, act and create my reality.* I create my pain through misalignment with my soul.

Item 9
Anatomy of Teen Purpose

Teen purpose is about igniting the passion and fire within that places them in a state of "thriving." This is what the late Dr. Peter Benson called "*sparks*... the innate and positive traits, interests and passions that every child needs help nurturing...and that sets them on a path of thriving." A teen that is on the path of thriving is filled with the following in their daily lives:

1. Hopefulness and optimism
2. Creativity and fulfillment
3. Engagement and contribution
4. Connection and happiness
5. Compassion, kindness and generosity
6. Passion and inspiration
7. Excitement for life and living, joy

Most Important Purpose Questions Teens Should Ask Themselves:

1. What brings me joy and fuels my energy and excitement for life?
2. What lights up my spirit and excites my interests?
3. What do I aspire to and what gives my life meaning?
4. What am I doing when I feel this way?
5. Am I willing to move toward the things that ignite a fire within me - using all of my creativity, passion, love and energy?

Areas That Ignite Teens Passions, Interests & Promote Thriving

According to the Search Institute research, some of the leading areas that ignite the inner "spark" of teens (gives joy, energy, fire, feeling of loving life and thriving) include:

- Music, dance, art and movement – this is the #1 area teens report giving their life hopefulness and fullness.
- Stewardship to the planet
- Subject area interests and sports
- Expression of inner qualities – i.e., kindness, compassion, understanding, etc.

Creating Environments That Allows Teens to Thrive – The Challenge & Opportunities

- Scientific studies have shown that in the US alone, 20% of the nearly 42 million youth experience depression. This means over 8 million of our youth are feeling lost, unfulfilled, hopeless, disconnected, disengaged, confused and helpless.
- Devastating Outcomes - We will lose the contributions of 8 million amazing minds and beings (who were meant to give to our world in meaningful ways) if collectively we don't do our part to ignite the unique fire and interests of our young people within our families, community, working environments and world.

Item 10
Teens & Adult Purpose - Differences

Adult and teen purpose functions somewhat differently. If you are a teen or parent of a teen, it is highly advised that you use a much lighter version of the "6 Steps." Use it mainly as a guide for reflection, conversation and learning, as opposed to an elaborate exercise. Gifting teens with the ability to be reflective about their talents, overcoming limitations and their importance to the world is invaluable! Differences:

1. Adults are already well on their path of life. Teens are just entering the path for creating their beautiful future. Therefore, they don't yet have a full spectrum of life experiences from which they are able to learn and cultivate information from. Don't expect teens to have all the answers right now.
2. Teens are learning to regulate, cultivate and exercise their creative abilities and regulatory stamina (emotions, thoughts).
3. Teens are undergoing a unique internal/external transformation process that completely renovates the structure and function of the brain and body. This affects a great deal about how they think, feel and act. Let them know it's normal!

(For more information on Teens, read "Your Amazing Itty Bitty Parenting Teens – 15 Powerful Strategies for Understanding How Your Teen Thinks.")

Gaining A New Perspective

The single most important thing is to *reveal the light, spark and joy of every human soul and to allow this to be expressed into the world.* Sadly, this is being shut off for our teens. We rarely ask our young people what inspires them, what gives them joy for life and living. Instead we train them to be test-takers, compete with one another and point out everything they do wrong. Rarely do we spend time discussing and cultivating their inner heart's desires. The following are constructive ways to view (and discuss) teen purpose.

- You are an ignited flame that needs to shine a specific light upon the world in only a way that you can do it!
- It's about bringing what's inside of you **out** into the world. What do you want to share, express? This can also include intangibles like bringing joy, connection, bridging diversity or creating peace.
- It's about today – and living joyfully and inspiringly in the "now."
- Teens are on the path to cultivating their talents, interests and heart's desires that will eventually **lead them** to their life's purpose. Each experience is a stepping-stone, which leads them toward their exhilarating, fulfilling and joyful life.

Item 11
You Are Not Your Emotions

From the full perspective of your total human design (mind, body and spirit), emotions are simply a technology, which acts as a guidance system to direct you. So often people *think* they are what their emotions are telling them. This couldn't be further from the truth! Here's what emotions do and are *telling* you when you listen.

1. Help you determine how far *off* or how *correctly aligned* you are with the perspective of your Soul (Higher Self or Spirit). The better you feel, the greater the alignment.
2. If you are authentically feeling the highest of human emotions (love, joy, gratitude, inspiration, compassion, peace, forgiveness, faith, etc.) you are completely and perfectly aligned with your Higher Self's perspective.
3. If you are feeling lower levels on the guidance system (fear, worry, guilt, blame, victimization, powerlessness, anger, stress, etc.), your thoughts and perspective are misaligned with your Higher Self's on the subject, person or experience at hand.
4. Emotions *assist* you in navigating life's experiences with greater stability, clarity and effectiveness!

*For a complete emotional scale (22 incremental emotions from high to low), google Abraham-Hicks Emotional Guidance Scale.

What You Can Do

Poorly regulated or misinterpreted emotions are often the cause of stagnation and roadblocks to your success, feeling good and flourishing. Here are a few tips for managing emotions.

- Get rid of *fear-based and limited* thinking! Thoughts have vibrations and quantum physics is now proving that we create realities through our thoughts – good or bad.
- Select upward thoughts and emotions. Invest wisely in what you choose to think, say and believe about yourself.
- Lighten up and don't take yourself so seriously! Do your best to add humor and levity to life's lessons and experiences. A joyful brain/mind is a resilient brain/mind!
- Use proper discernment and common sense. There are times when real fear is an appropriate response. Too often, however, we create fearful reactions and stress. Stress is harmful and corrosive to the mind and physical body. It's a purpose joy-kill!

Affirmations for Regulating Emotions

- "I AM not my emotions. They are only a technology to guide me."
- "I Am willing to allow myself to feel___ (joy, peace, confidence, love, forgiveness, etc.) now."
- "I AM willing to look at this from the perspective of my Higher Self."

Item 12
Beliefs & Imprints – Activating Internal Cooperation & Realignment

There are two critical things that help or hinder the flow of your life and pursuit of purpose: 1) what you believe and 2) what you say about yourself and your possibilities. Rather than aligning thoughts and words to the lower aspects of your ego (which hides you from the truth of your Soul), it will serve you much better to align and listen to your Higher Self – the highest aspect of your nature. Here's how beliefs work.

1. Beliefs aren't real. We only think they are real (or truths) because of our repetitive thoughts about them.
2. Most beliefs and thought patterns get hard-wired into our brains from 0-6 years from input received from our parents and surroundings. These become automatic, i.e., you don't think about them, they just happen (like walking, talking, etc.).
3. New beliefs and thought patterns can be changed at any time! All it takes is our conscious desire and attention to do so. This means you can change the circuitry of your own brain and program it for something different – something better! All you do is change your ***thoughts*** about the subject at hand. What you think about, you get!

The Anecdote – Affirmations

Telling a different story to the brain and mind (through affirmations) is one of the simplest ways to reprogram the brain, emotions and sub-conscious automatic belief patterns which hold you back from a fulfilling life. It is a triple bang for your effort! Affirmations do the following:

- Help rewire your brain to think, react and respond differently.
- Make powerful positive suggestions that the subconscious acts upon, helping create a life crafted according to the quality of the suggested impressions from your thoughts, emotions and feelings.
- Can change internal patterns by focusing on what you **do want** or like instead of what you don't. Remember, whether you think you can or you can't…. you are right! The Law of Attraction ensures that experiences match your thoughts, words and emotions. If you want a better life, it begins with better thoughts and stories.

Sample Affirmations

- I choose to believe differently about myself and this situation for the better!
- I AM powerful and release the illusion that I am a victim of anything or anyone.
- I step into the greatest version of myself now! I AM confident that I can change.

Item 13
How to Get Into Alignment with Your Higher Self

Connecting with your Spirit requires you to find and form a deeply connected relationship with the best part of you. This part of you is a spark of the Creator's (God or Source) essence within you, which expresses itself as your Higher Self, Spirit or Soul. It knows the truth about your true nature including your:

1. Undeniable value to this planet, as you were born for an important reason and with an indisputable purpose that is unique to your Soul.
2. Power to create and completely alter the circumstances of your life.
3. Limitlessness and inherent divine capabilities to experience perfect health, love, and possess bliss, compassion, kindness, peace and forgiveness in this physical lifetime.
4. True capacity for sustaining joy, no matter the circumstances you face in the classroom of life.
5. Your inexhaustible Light and abilities.
6. Unfaltering path to abundance and each step and turn to take you there.
7. Unshakable strength and confidence that comes forth as a product of identifying with your Divine nature.

Spirit & Purpose

Spirit isn't something outside of you. It IS you! You don't "find" something that you already possess. You simply listen to that which is already yours. Rules of understanding:

- Every human being came into this time-space reality with the intent to expand and live a joyful and meaningful life. You knew you had the internal equipment to achieve this before you were even born.
- The disharmony that you feel is a byproduct of not living in alignment with the original plan that your Soul intended.
- When we feel pain and dissatisfaction, it's simply that we aren't listening to the messages and callings of our own Soul – the bigger part of ourselves that knows the direction we were born to go and <u>what areas need developing along the way</u> in order to prepare us for the fullness of our roles and contributions.

How to Align with Spirit or the Higher Self

- Our Inner Being is never a victim of anything. It never operates in fear.
- It always chooses the higher road and the highest good for all.
- The Higher Self never screams, it only whispers to us when our mind is quiet.
- Whatever your area of struggle, the opposite is your opportunity for change!

Item 14
The Roadblock to Your Greatness

So what is getting in the way of your roadmap to happiness and stopping you from fully engaging in life and the full expression of your purpose? The human ego. Characteristics of human ego:

1. It is the antithesis of the Higher Self or your Divine nature. Imagine if you had a lever that moved from high to low. The Higher Self would be on the high end and the ego would be at the bottom. Which one do you tune into?
2. Ego is the imaginary mental voice that tries to trick and make us feel powerless, fearful and helpless at every turn. *It seeks to disconnect and hide us from experiencing and knowing the powers and truth about our true divine human nature, abilities and purpose.*
3. It is an aspect of human personality - one that is meant to be overcome and mastered. When this is accomplished, you learn to tune into the truth and wisdom of your real internal master, the Higher Self. Ego always creates a lot of noise, fear and chaos to divert attention away from the calm, silent presence and truth of the Higher Self, which patiently waits for us *to tune into ITS wisdom*

How Do I Know If Ego Is Running The Show?

When the ego is hard at work, it loves to pull you backward by distracting you into worrying about the future, lamenting over the past, or allowing you to get lost in a foggy chaos and hopeless cloud of lower energies and emotions such as:

- Fear, worry, stress, anger and resentment
- Judgment, guilt and unworthiness
- Lack, envy, jealousy and insecurity
- Hate, isolation and powerlessness

Tips for Overcoming the Ego

- Don't buy into it! None of it is true. You are a powerful creator (as we all are) and have the ability to direct your emotions, and achieve your heart and Soul's desires.
- Never dislike or go to war with the ego. That's just another way ego tries to get you to perpetuate lower emotions like anger, hate and resentment.
- Use your emotional technologies and the guidance scale often. (Item 11). Mentally polarize yourself on the high end – where your Higher Self resides.
- Quiet the noise and racing thoughts of the mind. This is ego. Regular, purposeful deep breathing, meditation, or the preparation activity in Item 2 are all *excellent* techniques to regain focus and connection with your Higher Self…. while quieting the ego.

Item 15
Getting Organized

After completing the exercises within this book, you're likely to have acquired insights about your purpose, and are perhaps unsure of what to do next. If you are missing clarity, this chapter will help you with that task. Here are a few tips.

1. Do the activities within this book in a state of joy and excitement. Do **not** approach them like doing an assignment or a checklist that has to "get done." *Fill the experience with beauty and appreciation for all that you are and all that you are becoming!* That is what purpose is all about. You are trying to bring forth *the true essence of YOU* through your loving attention to yourself and the exercises within this book. Your life is a process of moving *toward* your purpose.
2. Be patient. Sometimes the full revelation takes time to reveal itself. For example, I didn't get *full* clarity on my primary purpose until I was in my late 30's.
3. Reflect nonjudgmentally.
4. Put yourself into a mental frame of mind of joyful excitement and anticipation for the discovery and unveiling of the real and full expression of YOU.

Goal Setting & Tips

It's ideal to reflect upon your purpose *before* you feel pain and struggles caused by ignoring the callings of your Soul and not fully participating in the amazing life that was planned for you. When you are in alignment with the flow of your own life, you are in the flow of purpose!

- Keep your purpose sacred and to yourself. Let your actions (not words) broadcast.
- Keep it simple. Don't get overwhelmed. Pick 1-3 goals for yourself. Set objectives for what you want to accomplish. For example, if your goal is to *overcome fear*, break it down. Maybe begin by working on your fear of one unhealthy belief system. Once that is accomplished, branch out into other areas of fear. In reality, when you work on one area, it helps the others automatically!
- Don't force Step #6. If clarity about your life purpose isn't clear yet, be patient. Force is a repellent to clarity. Have *faith*.
- Use your imagination and daydream about what it would feel and look like to be living in your purpose. What are you doing that brings you joy and inspiration? Where are you and who are you working with? Live as though it has already happened! The Law of Attraction will act upon your mental images and feelings to draw it closer to you quicker.

You've finished. Before you go…

Tweet/share that you finished this book.

Please star rate this book.

Reviews are solid gold to writers. Please take a few minutes to give us some itty bitty feedback.

ABOUT THE AUTHOR

Gretchen is a Prevention Expert in Children, Teen and Adult Health, Conscious Parenting, Human Potential and Purpose Education; #1 Best Selling Author; CEO of Mind Body Spirit Parenting and founder of TheKidWhisper.com

As a 25-year veteran in the areas of applied neuroscience, behavioral nutrition, substance abuse, eating disorders, human physiology, physical/emotional/social school health and spiritual science, Gretchen creates a multifaceted holistic approach to affect change in paradigms for children, teens and adults by teaching people how to effectively utilize their human technologies of mind, body and spirit to improve every aspect of life, health and the human experience.

Gretchen has spoken locally and nationally on children and adult health topics. Her programs have been featured in the LA Times, CNN Health, Parent Magazine, on Los Angeles area news channels, Blue Zones Project, IDEA and her school health initiatives have received national recognition from the Alliance for a Healthier Generation.

For more information about Gretchen, conscious parenting topics or to obtain a copy of her comprehensive parenting guidebook "Mind Body Spirit Parenting Guidebook – Developing the Conscious Child," visit:

www.TheKidWhisper.com

**If You Liked This Book
You Might Also Enjoy…**

- **#1 Best Seller, Your Amazing Itty Bitty® Parenting Teens Book** – Gretchen E. Downey

- **Your Amazing Itty Bitty® Hypnosis** – Amy Mayne Robinson

- **Your Amazing Itty Bitty® Family Leadership Book** – Jacqueline Huynh Schaeffer

    With many more Amazing Itty Bitty® Books available in paperback and online…

www.ingramcontent.com/pod-product-compliance
Lightning Source LLC
Chambersburg PA
CBHW061304040426
42444CB00010B/2518